Changing Direction

by Natalie Hyde

Crabtree Publishing Company

www.crabtreebooks.com

Author
Natalie Hyde

Publishing plan research and development
Reagan Miller

Editors
Kathy Middleton
Reagan Miller

Proofreader
Crystal Sikkens

Notes to adults
Reagan Miller

Design
Katherine Berti

Photo research
Katherine Berti
Crystal Sikkens

Prepress technician
Ken Wright

Print coordinator
Margaret Amy Salter

Photographs
BigStockPhoto: pages 20, 24
Shutterstock: photo.ua: page 7; Foto011
Thinkstock: pages 15, 18
Other images by Shutterstock

Library and Archives Canada Cataloguing in Publication

Hyde, Natalie, 1963-, author
    Changing direction / Natalie Hyde.

(Motion close-up)
Includes index.
Issued in print and electronic formats.
ISBN 978-0-7787-0528-4 (bound).--ISBN 978-0-7787-0532-1 (pbk.).--
ISBN 978-1-4271-9017-8 (html).--ISBN 978-1-4271-9021-5 (pdf)

    1. Motion--Juvenile literature. 2. Force and energy--Juvenile
literature. I. Title.

QC133.5.H926 2014   j531'.11   C2014-900794-9
                                             C2014-900795-7

Library of Congress Cataloging-in-Publication Data

Hyde, Natalie, 1963- author.
  Changing direction / Natalie Hyde.
      pages cm -- (Motion close-up)
  Includes index.
  ISBN 978-0-7787-0528-4 (reinforced library binding : alk. paper) -- ISBN 978-
0-7787-0532-1 (pbk. : alk. paper) -- ISBN 978-1-4271-9021-5 (electronic pdf :
alk. paper) -- ISBN 978-1-4271-9017-8 (electronic html : alk. paper)
  1. Motion--Juvenile literature. 2. Force and energy--Juvenile literature. I.
Title.

QC133.5.H93 2014
531'.6--dc23
                                        2014004183

Crabtree Publishing Company

Printed in Canada/012017/TR20161124

www.crabtreebooks.com   1-800-387-7650

Published in Canada
Crabtree Publishing
616 Welland Ave.
St. Catharines, Ontario
L2M 5V6

Published in the United States
Crabtree Publishing
PMB 59051
350 Fifth Avenue, 59th Floor
New York, New York 10118

Published in the United Kingdom
Crabtree Publishing
Maritime House
Basin Road North, Hove
BN41 1WR

Published in Australia
Crabtree Publishing
3 Charles Street
Coburg North
VIC 3058

Contents

The world in motion

Motion is movement. Things are in motion all around us all the time. Objects need energy to move. This energy is called a **force**. Without a force, nothing would move.

A force can be a **push** or a **pull**.

A push moves an object away.

A pull brings an object closer.

What do you think?

Is this a push or a pull force?

How do you know?

5

Are all forces the same?

Every push and pull is different. Some pushes are strong. Others are weak. A strong push will make something move farther or faster. A tugboat can push a huge cruise ship.

A horse can create a strong pull.

It can pull a heavy wagon.

From one place to another

Forces also have direction. Some forces move things up or down. Other forces move things to the left or right. Some forces move things on a slanted line, called a **diagonal**.

What do you think?

Hot gas in a rocket creates a strong force. In which direction will this force push the rocket?

9

How does motion change?

A push or a pull makes an object start to move. An object will keep moving in a straight line unless a new force acts on it. Another force will make the motion of the object change.

What do you think?

Will this kick change the ball's motion? How do you know?

Let's get going!

Nothing will move without a pushing or pulling force. A ball on the ground will not move until a force moves it. A throw is a pushing force that moves a ball forward.

Wind is a force. It can push a beach ball through the air. Your body also has force. If you lift something, you are pulling it up.

Stop!

It takes a force to stop something that is moving. You can push something to make it stop. When you catch a football, you are using a pushing force to stop the ball.

You can also pull something to make it stop. If you pull on a dog's leash when he is trying to run, he will stop.

Faster and slower

Force can change the **distance** and **speed** that an object moves. Distance is how far something travels. Speed is how fast something moves. The stronger the force the farther the distance an object travels.

What do you think?

This girl wants to move the ball a short distance to the hole. Should she use a strong or a weak force?

Fast objects can move farther distances in a short amount of time. The harder the rider pushes his or her foot against the ground, the faster the skateboard will move.

When two objects touch

All things move in a straight line unless they are pushed or pulled from a different direction. A bumper car changes direction when it hits the side of another car. The bumper car might get pushed backward. It might bounce off in a new direction.

What do you think?

This baseball is moving in a straight line. How will the ball's motion change when it is hit with the bat?

19

Which way will it move?

The way objects **collide**, or bump into each other, decides how their direction changes. A bowling pin hit straight on by a ball is pushed backward. A pin hit on its left side will move right. A pin hit on its right side will move left.

The speed at which objects collide will also decide how their motion changes. A bowling ball that is moving slowly makes the pins fall over gently. A fast-moving ball has more force. It will knock the pins out of the way.

Moving and changing

We can see force changing motion all around us. Some objects start to move faster. Some change direction. Some come to a stop.

What do you think?

How does the motion of a puck change during a hockey game?

Words to know and Index

collide 20, 21

diagonal 8

force 4, 5, 8, 9, 10, 12, 13, 14, 16, 17, 21, 22

motion 4, 10, 11, 18, 21, 22, 23

pull 5, 6, 7, 10, 12, 13, 14

push 5, 6, 9, 10, 12, 13, 14, 16, 17, 18

speed 16, 21

24

Notes for adults and an activity

Help children understand how forces can change the direction of an object in motion. Demonstrate that the way to change the motion of an object is by applying a push or a pull.

• Take a walk around your neighborhood. Encourage children to take notice of the different plant life around them, from grasses and bushes to flowers and trees.

• **Be a Plant (and planet) Protector!**
Use the information from this book and the resources listed here to learn how to protect and preserve plants and other natural resources. Help children create an online posting or use recycled paper to make a poster sharing their important message.

Learning more

Books
Give it a Push! Give it a Pull! A Look at Forces by Jennifer Boothroyd, Lerner Classroom, 2010.
How Does it Move? by Bobbie Kalman, Crabtree Publishing, 2009.
Move It!: Motion, Forces and You by Adrienne Mason, Kids Can Press, 2005.

Websites
At eSchoolToday learn all about forces and how they change motion.
http://eschooltoday.com/science/forces/ introduction-to-forces.html
Hubpages talks about force and how it can change the direction of an object.
http://joanca.hubpages.com/hub/ Learn-About-Motion-and-Force-for-Kids